Go & Dot: Transportation on the Go

by Happy Kids Press

A TRACTOR TRAILER DRIVING DOWN A HIGHWAY

A BIPLANE
FLYING IN THE SKY

A DUMP TRUCK
CARRYING A LOAD OF DIRT

A RACE CAR SPEEDING AROUND A TRACK

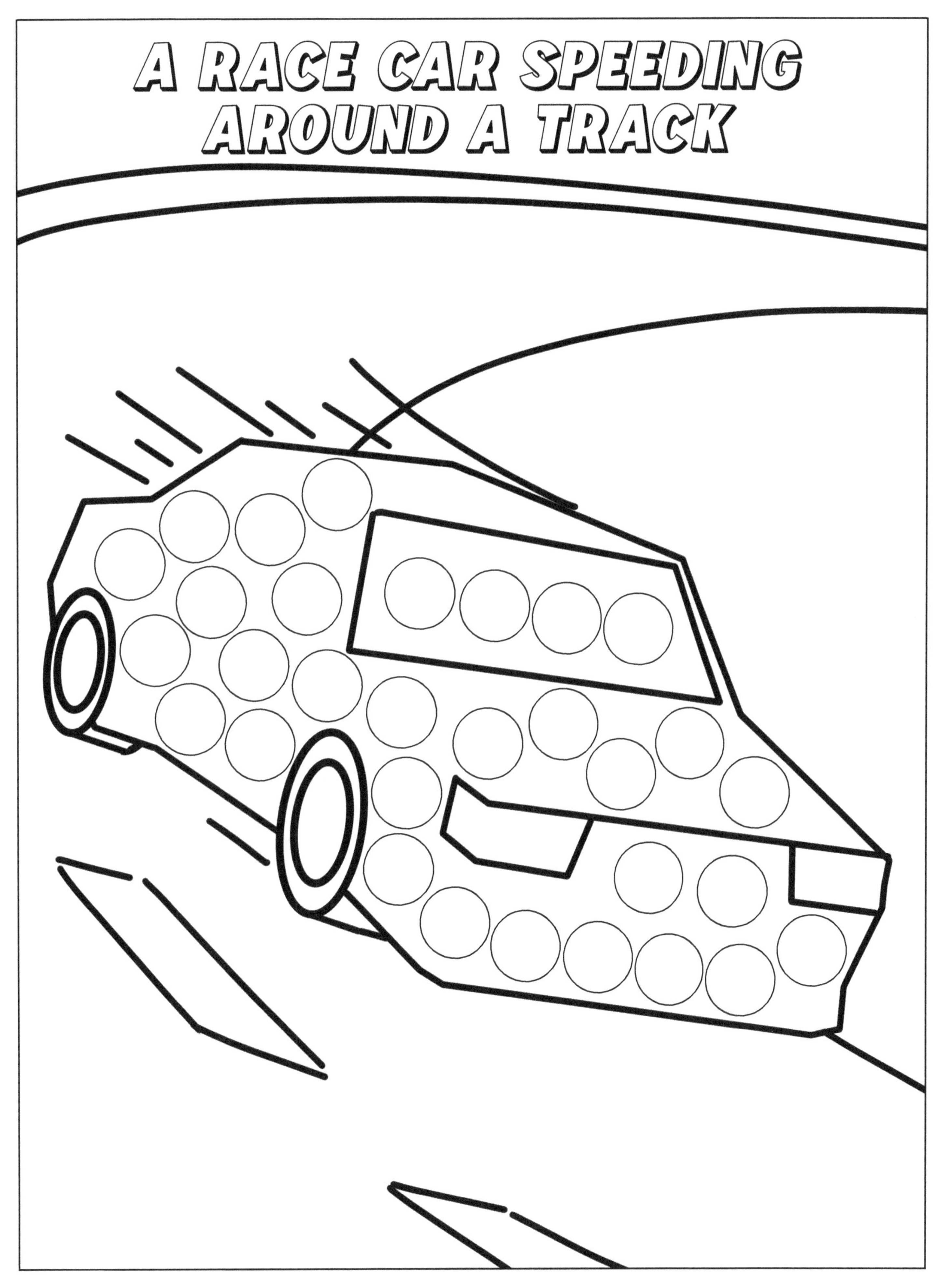

A MOTORBOAT
PULLING A WATER SKIER

A SNOWMOBILE RACING ACROSS A SNOWY LANDSCAPE

A CABLE CAR CLIMBING A STEEP HILL

A SNOWPLOW
CLEARING A SNOWY ROAD

A ROCKET BLASTING OFF INTO SPACE

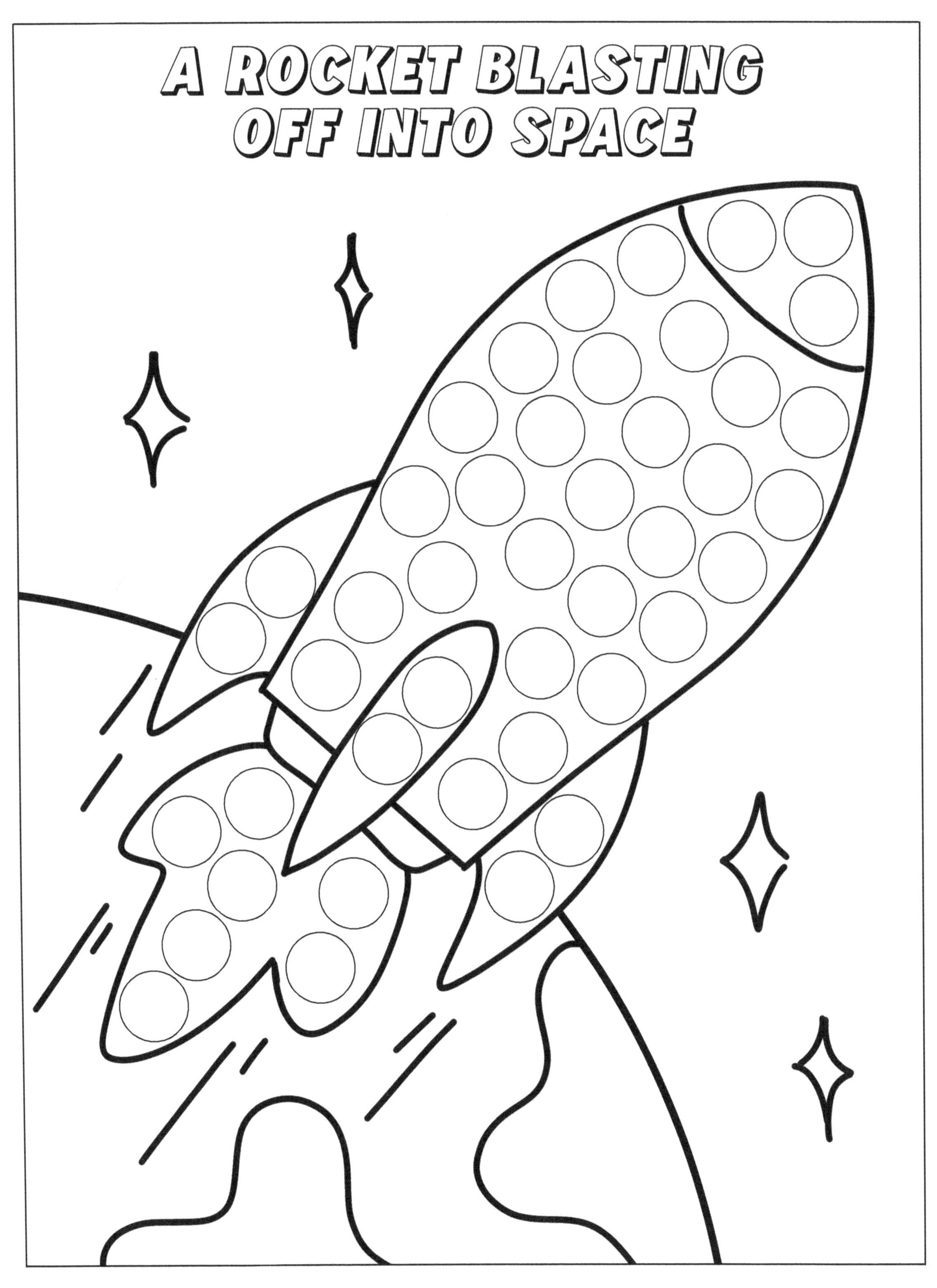

A SKATEBOARDER DOING TRICKS AT A SKATE PARK

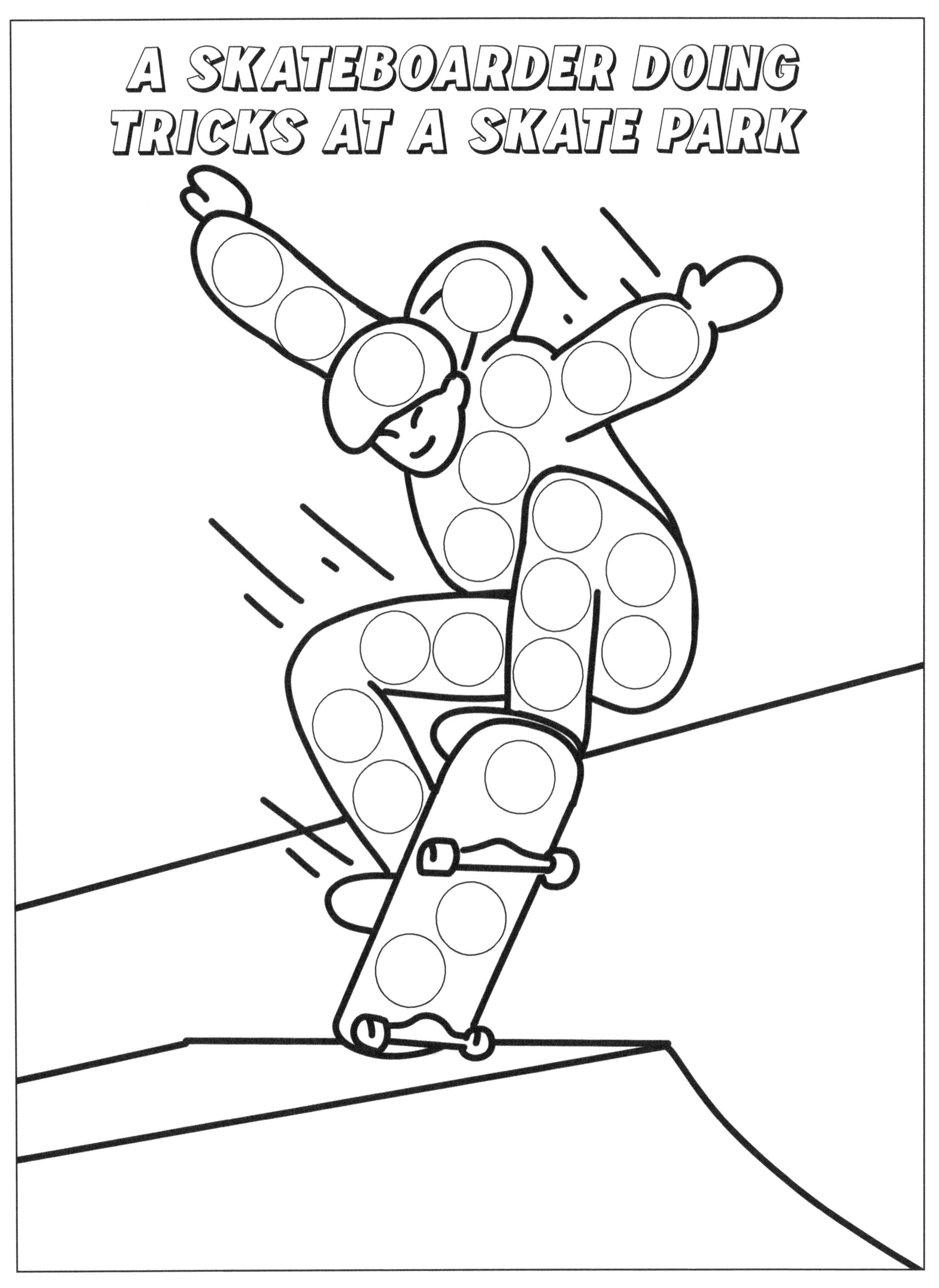

A SCHOOL BUS
PICKING UP STUDENTS

A HOT ROD CRUISING DOWN THE HIGHWAY

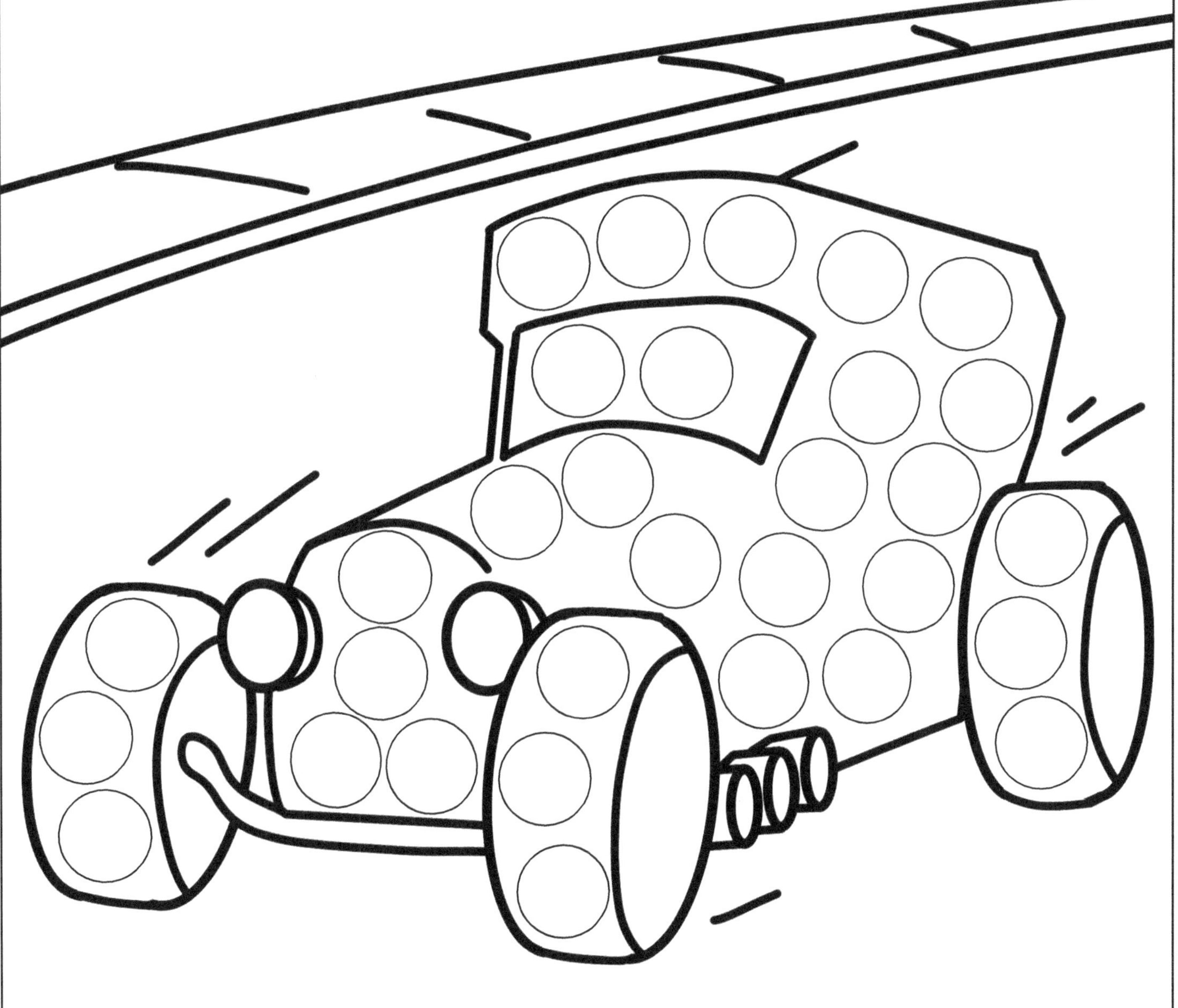

A ROLLER COASTER SPEEDING THROUGH TWISTS AND TURNS

A POLICE CAR CHASING
AFTER A ROBBER
POLICE

A SNOWBOARDER CARVING DOWN A MOUNTAIN

A DELIVERY TRUCK DROPPING OFF PACKAGES

A SPACE SHUTTLE
LANDING ON A RUNWAY

A BICYCLE RIDING DOWN A COUNTRY ROAD

A FIRE TRUCK RUSHING TO PUT OUT A FIRE

A JET FLYING
HIGH IN THE SKY

A SPEEDBOAT RACING ACROSS A LAKE

A JET SKI SKIMMING OVER THE WATER

A HELICOPTER HOVERING IN THE AIR

AN ICE CREAM TRUCK
PARKED BY A PARK

A POLICE HELICOPTER HOVERING OVER A CITY

A BLIMP FLOATING IN THE SKY

A FORKLIFT MOVING HEAVY BOXES

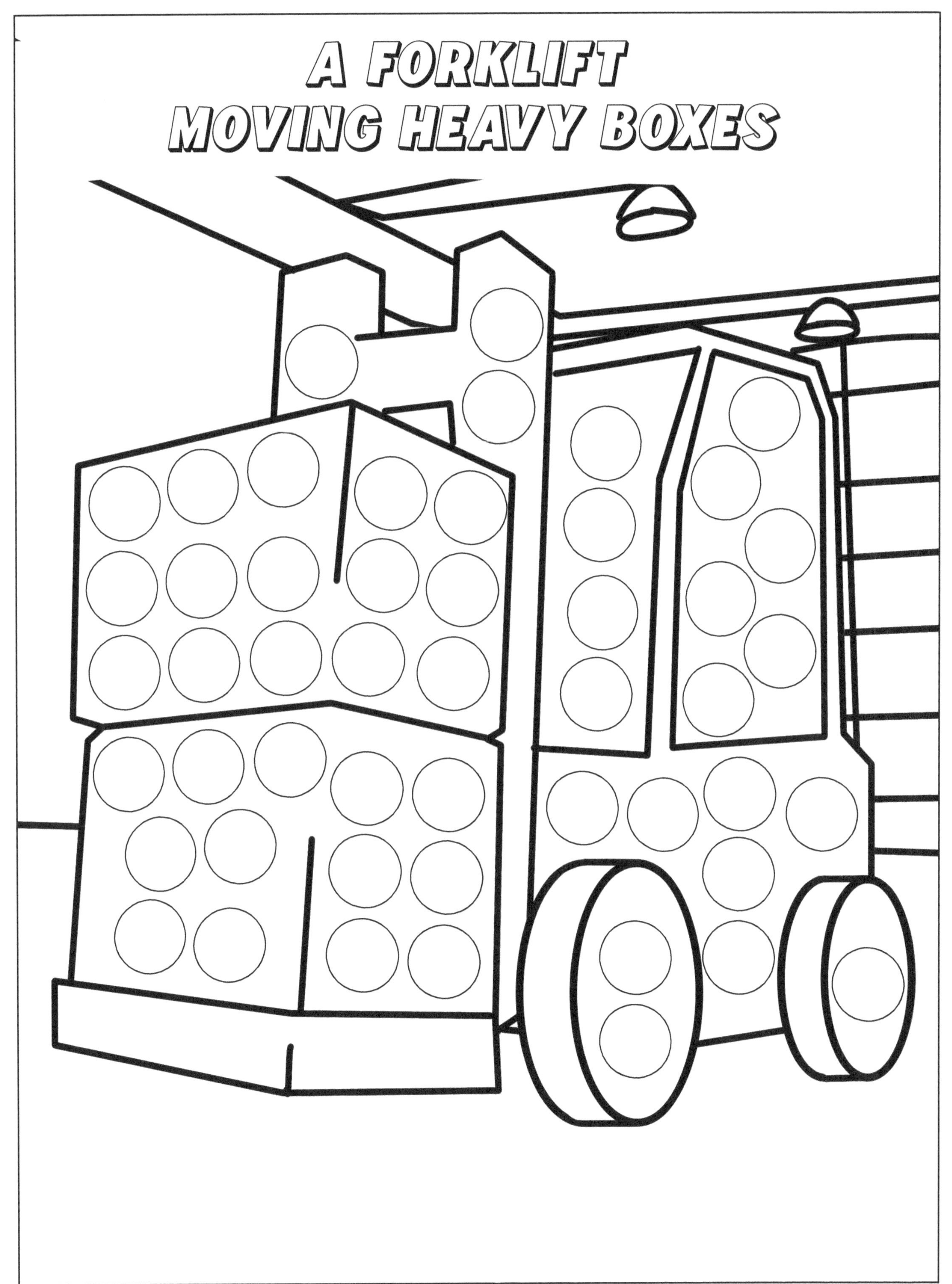

A MOTORCYCLE ZOOMING DOWN THE ROAD

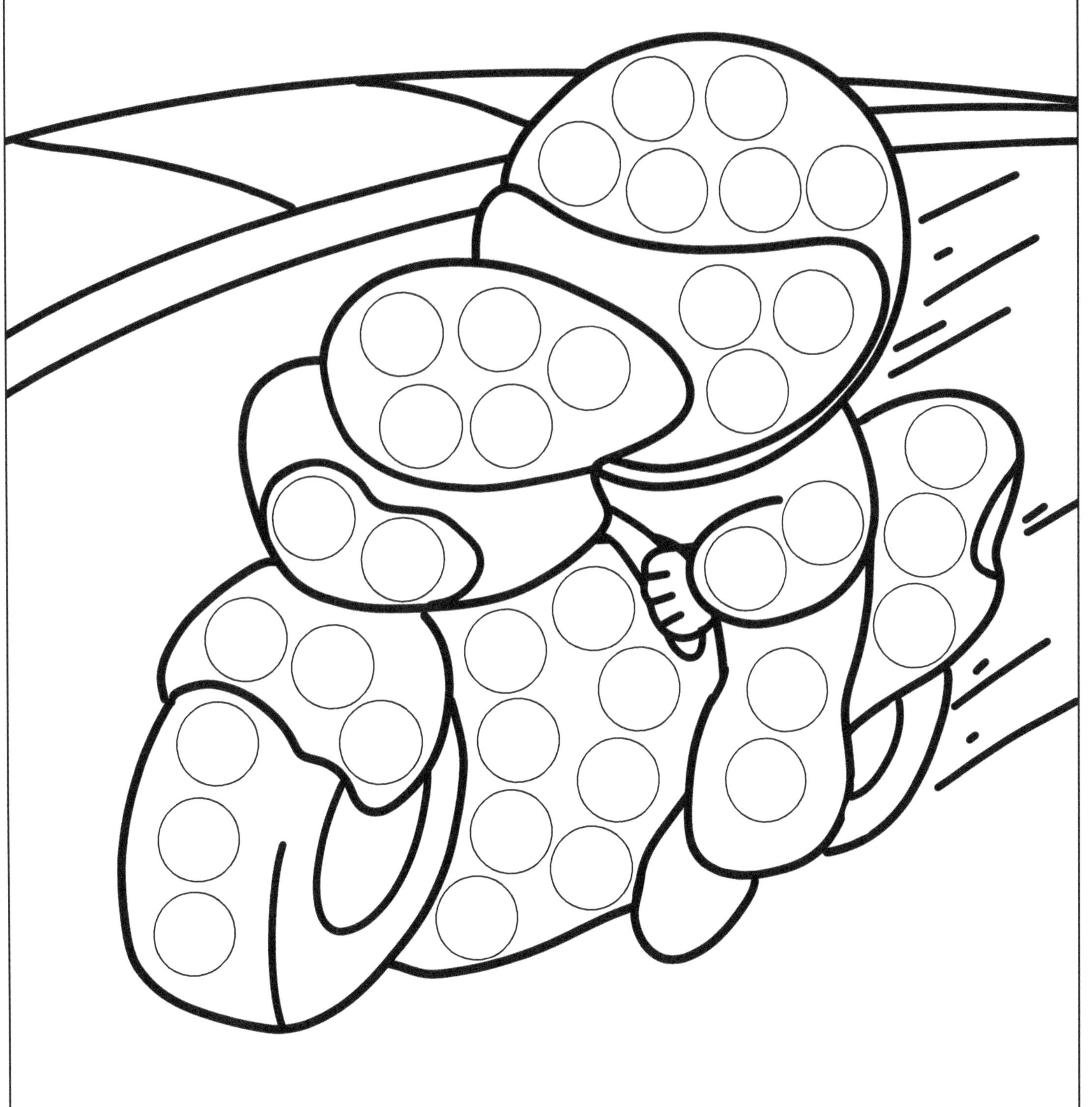

A PIRATE SHIP SAILING ON THE OPEN SEAS

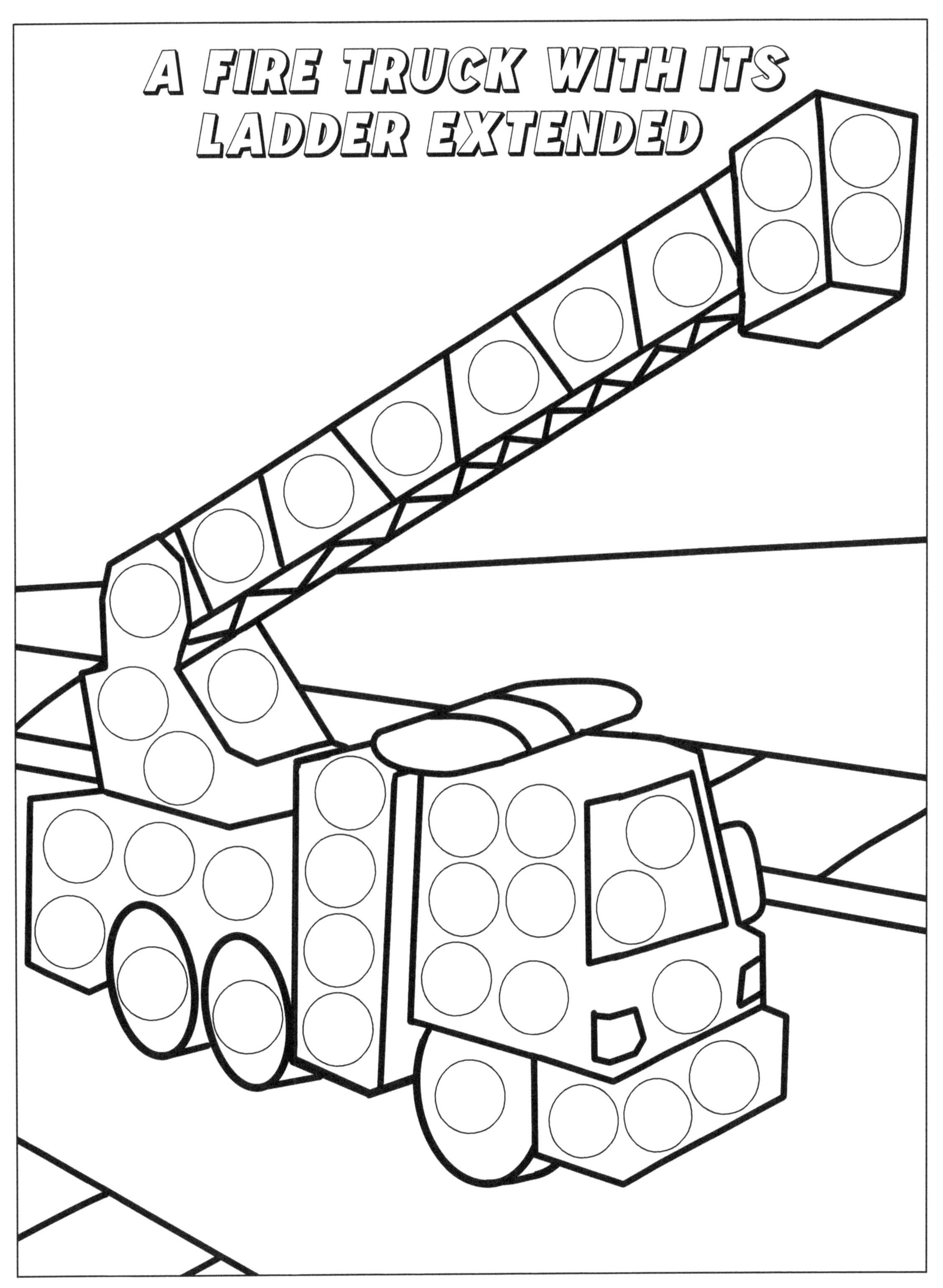

A FIRE TRUCK WITH ITS
LADDER EXTENDED

A GARBAGE TRUCK COLLECTING TRASH

A MONSTER TRUCK CRUSHING CARS

A BUS FULL OF HAPPY PASSENGERS

A HOT AIR BALLOON FLOATING IN THE SKY

A TRAIN CROSSING
A TALL BRIDGE

A HORSE-DRAWN CARRIAGE IN A PARK

A SUBMARINE DIVING DEEP INTO THE OCEAN

A BOAT SAILING ON A CALM LAKE

A TRAIN CHUGGING THROUGH
A MOUNTAIN TUNNEL

A CAR DRIVING THROUGH A RAINBOW

A FOOD TRUCK
PARKED AT A FESTIVAL

A TAXI DRIVING THROUGH A BUSY CITY

A TRACTOR PLOWING A FIELD

A VINTAGE CAR PARKED IN FRONT OF A CLASSIC DINER

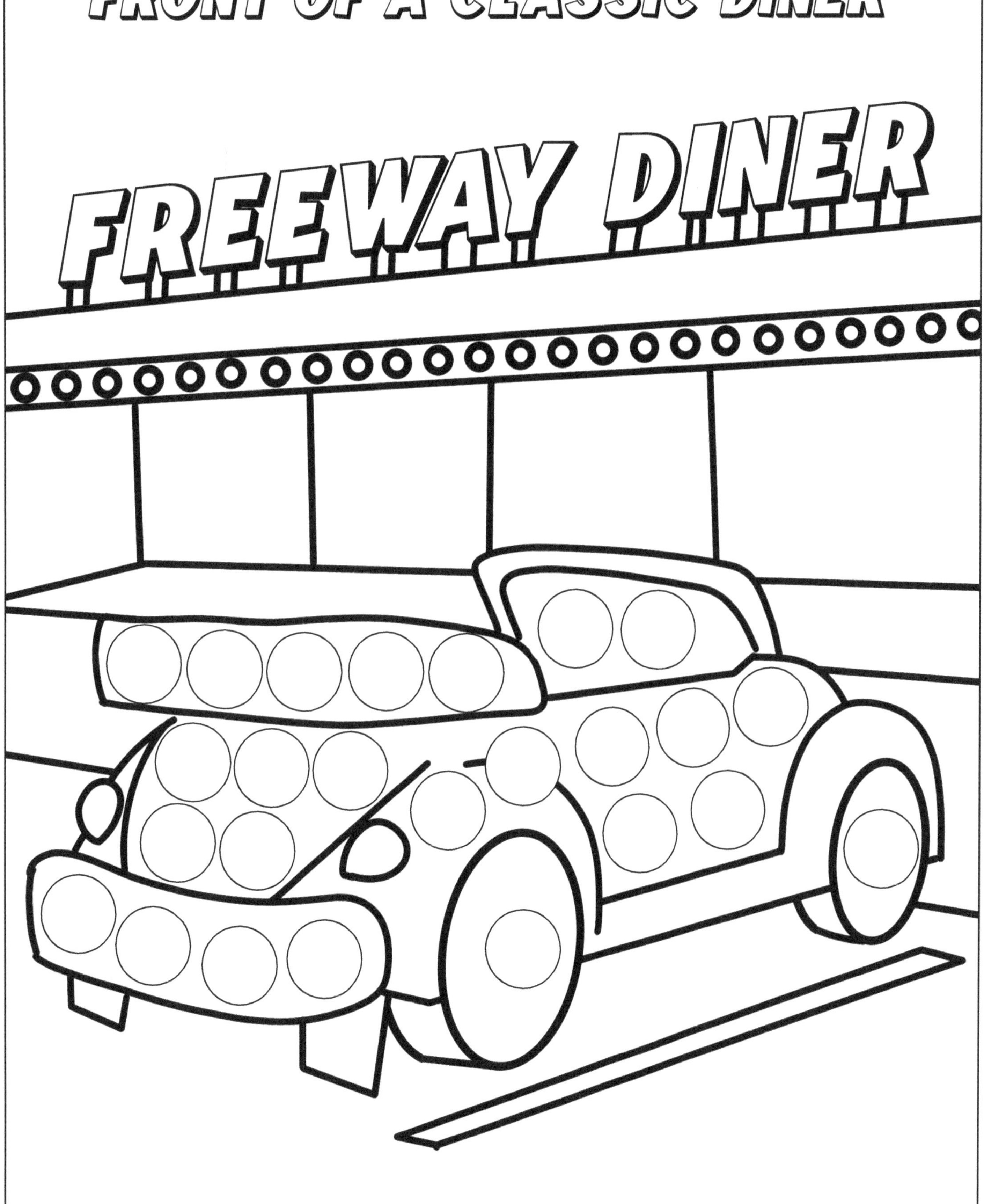

A GONDOLA FLOATING DOWN A CANAL

A SAILBOAT GLIDING ON A CALM OCEAN

A TUGBOAT PULLING A BARGE

A BULLDOZER CLEARING A CONSTRUCTION SITE

A SURFBOARD RIDING A BIG WAVE

A CAR DRIVING THROUGH A FIELD OF FLOWERS